_____

_____

_____

Joy

Wandering around streets we've never seen before, taking in new sights, sounds and smells. Bundled up in winter coats. Madrid, Spain, Vancouver, Canada. The walking, the cool air, the clear skies — so exhilerating. So many things in this world to experience.

Complex Joy —

At school, where I love to be, this person disrupts my feelings of joy. A fly in the otherwise perfect ointment. Her instability, unpredictibility, hostility. Ugh. Why did I cover up her misdeeds. Now she's here for good?

What brings me joy?

- My love
- Our cats
- Our home
- Our plants
- Books
- Music
- My parents
- My siblings
- My nephew
- My neice
- My friends
- Yoga
- Time alone
- Time with friends
- New places
- Planning a trip
- Chilly weather
- Fresh sheets
- Fresh towels

- Daylight savings time
- Christmas lights
- Stability
- Financial security

Complicated Joy Situations

- D.A.
- D.B.
- Multiple Sclerosis
- Break up in '96
- ↑ and ↓ weight
- Coming out
- Aging parents
- Inlaws in town
- Long flights to faraway places
- Tests
- Gray hair
- Dr. Match

May my time in the car with my dad bring us mutual joy.

May my teaching history bring me joy and inspire the kids to love learning about our past.

May each book I read bring me the joy of discovery.

May each trip I take in the future bring me the joy of discovery.

May even challenging behaviors at school bring me the joy of laughter.

May I cherish all of the time spent with my parents and Josephines parents as well. The time is limited and should be gathered as often as possible.

Made in the USA
Las Vegas, NV
13 June 2021

24668486R10069